We dedicate this book to all the voices that still need to be heard. We see you.

Preface

At Simply Youth Institute, we don't just equip young people for the future—we walk beside them as they uncover the leaders they were always meant to be. Still We Shine: Stories of Connection and Growth embodies that journey. It is a living, breathing testament to what happens when young adults are given the tools, the space, and the support to rise.

This collection was born from the intentional work of SYI's Workforce Readiness Internship Program, which supports college-aged students 18-24 from Lane County, Oregon, and Los Angeles, California, as they take their first bold steps into professional life. Through curated workshops, mentorship, hands-on projects, and community service, our interns gained far more than workplace skills—they discovered their voice and learned how to use it with power and purpose.

In this anthology, interns reflect on personal and professional transformation. They write through the lens of lived experience, sharing what it means to confront real-life challenges—educational struggles, identity questions, cultural pressures, mental health battles—and still show up, speak truth, and shine. These stories are not filtered or polished for perfection. They are raw, courageous, and full of heart because they are real. And real is what heals. Real is what connects us.

Our role at SYI has always been to create a space where young people can grow in knowledge, confidence, clarity, and calling. We intentionally design professional development that goes beyond resume-building. Students learn how to collaborate, lead, and communicate with empathy. They are trained to innovate, to own their impact, and to move through the world as change agents. This collection reflects that journey, page by page, story by story.

What you hold in your hands is far more than a book. It is something tangible that says, "I have a voice, and it matters." For these first-time authors, it proves that their stories have value and their perspectives have power. And for our readers, it is an invitation to listen, learn, and believe in the next generation of leaders shaping our communities.

Still We Shine is also a testament to the strength of collective progress. These stories were not written in isolation. They were birthed in community, crafted through mentorship, and shaped by peers walking parallel journeys. These young adults challenged each other, uplifted each other, and grew together. This kind of leadership lasts—leadership rooted in empathy, integrity, and shared purpose.

And yet, this book is only the beginning. These stories mark a decisive moment, but what comes next is even more critical. These future leaders will continue to build, heal, and ignite transformation in the world around them. They now move forward not only with skills and experiences but with the confidence that their voice can open doors for themselves and others.

To every young author in this collection: we see you, honor you, and are proud beyond words. And to our readers: welcome. May these pages stir something in you. May they challenge you to believe deeper, to listen closer, and to invest in youth potential like never before.

This is just the beginning. Still—we shine.

—The Simply Youth Institute Team

Jacob Long

A Sight of Sunshine

Everyday, when I head off to work
I see a man in the snow
tall, pale-white skin, a simple flannel, sweatpants and hat
standing there, silently
staring into the distance
almost like a ghost.

I never approach him
for he is not worth my time.
How would my friends react
to see me, an attractive wealthy man
with such a basic and dull creature?

When I get home
he's never there.
Not even a trace.
No footprints.
No marks.
Nothing.

I'm tired of this.

This morning I approach.
I will make sure he leaves
then I will never have to be in his filthy presence again.

If he notices I approach
he does not show it.
        Sir, why do you choose to bring yourself to this
neighborhood every morning?
        Look at these big houses, the beautiful parks, even
the clothes of the pedestrians!
        This place is not a place for you...

so, could you please stop coming here so much?

He doesn't respond for a very long time.
Just when I'm about to get angry
he speaks.
     I will leave when the time is right
     or maybe I will not
     why should it matter?
     For we are all but grains of sand
     shifting endlessly on this planet we call Earth
     no different from the next.
     We're always so quick to be carried off by the wind
or the ocean
     join the desert or beach
     but why don't we ever take the time to enjoy the
riverside?

What in the world did this weird man just say?
     What is this foolery?
     First of all, scram old man!
     And then take some lessons on speaking English!

He ignores me
     Here, just look at this sunrise.
     Watch how the darkness falls asleep after it's hard
night of work
     and the light takes over for it.
     Is it not just mesmerizing?

As I am about to lose it, I look up
and it captures me.
The light climbing over the horizon
the bright colors clashing with the dark blue sky
the rays appearing one by one
the stars flicker out thousands of miles away.

Such a simple thing
but so much depth behind it

Amazing

      I think the time is indeed right now.
      It was a pleasure to meet you.
I look back to see the man completely gone
but not only that
there's not even a trace.
No footprints.
No marks.
Nothing.

I have not seen the man once since that day
but everyday before work
I put on a flannel, sweatpants and hat
walk out from my house into the snow
and watch the sun rise.
Standing silently
staring into the distance

enjoying the moment.

Question 5: Adjusting to the Unknown

I remember a time that our parents assured us they would wait until we were moved out to divorce. Despite showing clear signs of being unhappy in their marriage, my parents led me and my two brothers to believe that they had our best interest in mind, and the difficulties of having split parents in childhood would never be something we would have to live through. But that notion unfortunately came crashing down when my parents sat us down in June of 2021 to tell us that our father would be moving out. The anger quickly consumed me at the time. I felt as if the trust between me and my parents had been shattered, and I had every right to be livid. But was this mindset truly valid? Through those first few months of my parents' divorce, I realized not only how self entitled and cruel my mindset had been towards my parents in their marriage, but also learned how unfair it was to expect that the important life choices made by my loved ones would revolve around my best interest alone.

Through the years growing up with my parents' marriage still intact, I hardly ever remember seeing them showing true affection towards each other. Every night would devolve into arguments, or sometimes screaming matches. The worst offense of this was on car rides, where I worried that whoever was behind the wheel would focus more on getting their point across than what was on the road ahead of them. I knew this wasn't normal. But I didn't care how unhappy my parents' lives had become as long as the Nintendo Wii on the fireplace shelf stayed where it was and I got to sleep in the same bed every night. A divorce would change those things, and I thought that was unacceptable.

But as the divorce was finalized and I got accustomed to the new system of spending about half of the week with my dad, those changes became something I had to learn to accept. It took a long time for his tiny two-room apartment to start feeling like a second home, the lack of privacy is something I still struggle with to this day. Something else that I picked up on, however, was the shift in behavior from both of my parents. My father became more eager to hear about our days after school than ever before,

and my mother had a general sense of calmness I rarely
saw from her before. For the first time in a long time, my
parents seemed genuinely happy, even if it was individu-
ally, and noticing this after a while was what led me to my
outlook in the present day. I realized that their happiness
reflected back onto me, and much of the initial anger had
dissipated. But what else clicked in my mind, was a far
greater lesson that I needed to learn.

As I look back on this period now, I've learned to
put myself in my parent's shoes and appreciate the effort
they have put into making me a happy student, athlete,
and son. My parents were very unhappy in their marriage,
but still fought to stay together for as long as they could to
give me a stable childhood. I now see how selfish I was in
thinking that they owed me more, when their marriage was
never about me in the first place. It's about them. They are
now much happier than they ever were while married, and
their happiness gives me much more joy than one single
roof over my head ever could. Using this lesson, I try to
be more cognizant of what the important people in my life
can do for themselves first rather than for me first. Because
after all, how can I expect anyone to want to help me when
I can't even let them help themselves?

Grieve.

What does it mean to love someone? For a long time I thought loving someone meant expressing your value for them in the form of actions and choices. The choice to dance with him in the rain knowing full well both of you could catch a cold, to hold her tightly in your arms as she cries through the finale of your favorite TV show, to sacrifice anything and everything to see a smile stretch across their face.

But what happens when you can't show that someone anymore? The time to express that value or make those choices isn't always guaranteed. That someone might have moved out of your life, might even be a new someone. You never really stop loving that someone. But how do you express value or make choices for someone who isn't there anymore? How do you love someone who's gone?

Well, you may not be able to dance with him in the rain anymore, but you can look back on when you did with sadness, joy, anger, appreciation that you participated in such a wonderful experience with them. Someone else might be holding her through each episode, but you can think about that with rage relief sorrow content knowing you got to be that shoulder to cry on for a time. That smile may never reach them from your actions again, but you can cry on the floor, write letters of fury, pour your heart out to your friends, live on knowing it once was.

The answer is to grieve, and to grieve properly. Grieve what you had and what could have been. Cry on the bathroom floor. Write so much in a journal you need a second one to hold all the anger. Talk with who will listen until your ice creams melt all over you and you have a new memory to laugh about.

There will come a day months or years down the line on a balmy Sunday afternoon when you're out in the rain after watching your favorite show with a big smile on your face and you'll realize; the urge to grieve for them has been gone for a long time. And that, that lack of emotion, lack of a hole in your heart, lack of anything when you hear their name in a passing conversation and carry on with your day like usual, that's when the love you had fades away along with them.

But you don't get there without embracing it. Embracing every wildly wacky painful emotion in the grieving process. If you love someone, whether present or not, whether they deserve it or not, you'll make that choice to express it however you please, whenever you please. To truly and properly grieve the loss of someone is to *prove* to yourself that you <u>loved.</u> So don't grieve for them, grieve for you. Because every time you grieve the heart that's no longer in your hands, you show yourself that you have the ability to cherish, to put someone beyond yourself, to love, and there is nothing that could be more beautiful.

Remember that.

The Allure Of A Stranger

I discovered you on a Tuesday afternoon, chatting quietly with your friend in sharp contrast with the exuberance of the little kids on the playground nearby. The chill autumn wind flows through your golden brown hair, and in moments of calm it rests behind you over the park bench. All it takes is one glance for your figure, your humanity to fill up my head completely, and to remove it now would be an impossible endeavor. Like a hardened cement that has completed its task. To solidify, and stand forever stationary where it lies. I continue moving, beyond you now, but I bring with me a new set of conclusions I can't help but jump to. A blur of moments spent together, a fantasy longing to be played out. A lifetime together, you and me.

I want to double back. Break the routine. Take an extra lap around the park today just to get one final view of you, and add fuel to my ever growing fire once more. What I would give for some benign blessing from the universe that would get you to stop me. You'd ask me where I was headed, or kindly point out that my shoe was untied. There's not a single logical reason for why you would, and in between my own makeshift cut-scenes about a perfect life together, my mind recognizes and respects this. There's no reason for you to stop me. There's no reason for you to care about me, or love me, or put the idea of my simple existence into your mind. Our paths were never meant to cross, and to try and force destiny, to play God and create something that shouldn't be, would be deeply selfish of me.

But all the same I am still forever thankful. Thankful that I was granted a moment of your allure, your presence, your beauty, and the joy they combined to present me with in simply getting to think about you. What truly should be celebrated is the acceptance of what is, not the lust of what could be more. So thank you, beautiful stranger. Thank you for blessing me with your image, your mystery of a life that I can now ponder upon with interest, and your beauty, that by simply observing from afar, granted me a wealth of happiness.

I turn the corner and run down my usual, old familiar world, thoughts still filled with the stranger, but with a little more room for what else might be beautiful.

The Letter I'll Never Send

I know. I know I'll never be able to show this to you no matter how much I want to. I know you'll never get to know how sorry I am, how sorry I am that I let things turn out the way they have. I'll always blame myself for not doing more, even if truly there was no more to be done.

I'll never be able to tell you how much I miss watching shows with you in your bedroom, laughing together as we eat lunch in my car, holding you close on all the cloudy days. I miss the you that you were, that you are, and that you'll become, and I'm sorry I didn't show those last two versions enough love. I pushed them away, I tried to morph and change them to my liking when that was never my decision to make, and in doing so I lost the one person who wanted to care for me the most.

I hope we can reconnect one day and try again. This time, I promise I'll be better. I'll love you how you deserve to be loved, and fill the faultiness I created before we find ourselves falling, faster, further, darker. In the meantime, all I can do is hope that you're happy. You deserve to be happy, make others happy, and let your joy radiate around you.

Even if I know I may never again feel that radiation.

Forgiveness

A night in vain
frigid and hollow
You gave me this pest
That feeds on my sorrow.

He trashes my room
He eats all my food
But I can't remove him
That task is on you.

I'm not fully confident you even know that he's here
No matter how many times I thought I made myself clear.
I can't believe you'd do this, just to leave me uncovered
Wish I knew from the start that these were your true
colors.

You won't take him back, but I don't deserve this
It just leaves me asking
Is this really worth it?

There's so much of my life that I have left to live
And this creature does not get to decide it
Regardless who stops the pain that he gives
All this sadness for me is unfit.

It's time to move on, and swallow my pride
I'm done letting myself get sucked in by the tides

I'm back on my path, the one that I knew
Now I'm able to say, knowing it's true…
That I truly and wholeheartedly forgive you.

Skyla Bird

Icarus

Candles melt their waxes to honor me,
The heavens beckon like a sirens call,
Daedalus I plea, help set me free,
Twas not I caused benevolent pitfall

Aliferous as the birds soar above,
Abvolating free from our confinements,
Mourning doves cry, alluding what's to come,
Adjusting wind to perfect refinement

Glide swift as the mighty owl I pray,
Life below shrinks to obsolete mundanes,
Soaring agape to thy heavens I pray,
Not prophecy nor tale can cause me strain

Faster, farther from ecstasy I fall,
"Did I fly too close to the sun?" I call

Robin's Song

Water droplets trickle over the stream bed,
A robin breathes in its song like the clean air around us,

but it's no longer clear

Smog fills the robins' lungs
		Breathe,

				Breathe,

						Breathe,

									Swell,
							Swell,

				Swell,
But just as the Earth's lungs,
		Its atmosphere,
		Its land is

				Swelling,

							Swelling,

Swelling,
swelling with smog

						people

							pollution
The robin's lungs are still.
		1
			2
				3
					BREATHE!

There I lay,
Breathing in the stagnant air of my propane household,
My seatherny staggers…
           Will it ever get better?

Blossoms

Sunlight breaks clouds open as it stretches its arms of light
out into blue sky,
A sense of hope fills the lungs of the air,
The apricity of warm sun creeps in through the crevasses of
the blinds,
Spring has come!

Children laugh,
Students sunbathe,
The world is defrosted

Dendrophiles become one with tree bark,
Climbing their way up the body of the evergreens,
          Even they need a little light
Heliophiliacs twirl in the sun rays,
Rain lovers admire the way fresh blossoms glow with lus-
ter,
Flora stretch their leaves, waving at passersby,
Campus is bustling.
Girl Scouts sell happiness and sweets,
Birds chirp at the warmth, serenading it to linger just a little
longer,
Students play hacky sack and slackline,
This is what campus is supposed to look like.

As the sun sets contentment remains,
We are one with the iris,
Opening up our dark patches to fill our souls with lumines-
cence,
Interconnected by invisible strings,
Invisible roots,
We are all blossoms

Drill, baby, drill

Dozens of bulldozers crowd the land,
Raiding it like kids swarming a pinata,
Ignorant and blissful with the hatchet in their hand,
Leading themselves like cows to their own slaughter
Land of liberty is dead

Bigots command the land with their dollar,
Antiscians reek of sweat while oligarchs stretch them far-
ther,
Bears scrape and suffer while the smoke plumes rise taller,
You all are the problem, none of you are martyrs

Day by day the countdown recedes,
Riddled by hate and privilege and greed,
I wonder; will our youth have land they can roam?
Light your own spark, find your way home
Land of liberty is dead.

Koi no yokan

A light hum of car engines drone in the air,
Parents call their children over to drive home,
We walk as a pair,
Thinking about what's to come, our eyes awkwardly roam,
I glance toward him, his hair shines against a background
of darkening sky,
We share a joke only us two would laugh at,
His chuckle as infectious as that time I had pink eye.

My alexithymia asphyxiates me,
If his eyes were akin to the stars above I'd practice sabaism
religiously,
The incalescence of his spirit warms our realm beneath the
cottonwood tree,
I feel a bit fidgety,
My instilled immerensis is all consuming; "why would he
choose me?"

He's sitting there empyreal,
I feel different,
Safe,
     Warm,
          Smiley
               Excited,
The Japanese would call this "koi no yokan"
The Chinese "yuanfen"
I call it belonging,
I call it love,
And this love will last,
Last as long as the stars shine above in the sky

Maija

The sweet smell of bear-grass and old wood rush my nos-
trils,
      Friends laughing,
      Gravel shuffling,
      Doors closing,
An essence of comfort swirls through the air,
A warm, calm smile of my past self
      Math,
      Havasupai,
      Damp morning dew on the field,
      Wheels turning in my head,
I long to be like Maija

Maija is sunshine
Her golden, shiny hair waving with the bear-grass,
The aroma of vellichor that seeps from the cracks of her
house itch at my senses,
Maija can do anything,
Maija is everything,
      The soft drip of rain after the monsoons,
      A wealth of knowledge as large as the Alexandria
Library,
      The bravery I reach for in the depth of the night
Her quiddity radiates hope

Maija,
      M
            A
                 I
                     J
                         A
Succinct in its letters but vast in its beauty,
A myriad of ways to spell her name,
But only one orthography is synonymous with her
So as I sit there,

Braiding the bear-grass that's as aureate as her hair,
Weaving through the valleys of my fingers,
I find hope in darkness…
If Maija can do anything,
I can do anything

Tree Hugger

Tried and true it towers above,
Roots sink deep, deep, deeper,
Elders cover the seedlings with love,
Ephemeral dashes of growth from the womb of Demeter

Hemlock and hawthorn and hickory alike,
Undergo the harkes of their past,
Gouging themselves open to house the migrating shrike,
Greeting those who bimble along, no longer steadfast,
Ever-changing, always constant,
Ridden with the nightmare of the sky

Anya Grabovski

Following summer
Again and again
Later in the year
Leaves blowing off a tree

Walking in the snow
It crunches as you go
Never so white
Talk of the town
Even birds would delight as they
Rest easy tonight

Summer close
Petunias blooming
Right in the glowing light
In from the sun
Near to the Earth
Getting back for Spring

Flowers

Hello, hello!
I love to see you
It's been a long winter,
But I am as happy as a cello!

Now who is this next to me?
Haven't I seen you before?
You look quite familiar,
My dear, where's your color?!

I struggled like a caterpillar
And came out of the ground
What a cold welcome
But I guess that's what happens
When you avoid the bee.

My stay is short
But I am saying hello
From above, I was sent below.
Just here to provide you support.

Poem on Existing

Structureless, stupid creatures.
Golden clocks,
Abundant in mighty, working ants who build their statures
Yet still floating not far from docks.
Dually going through the waves of time.

My Delectable Stew

When I am colored blue I resort to stew.
Sometimes with bread,
Accompanied with butter, I turn red.
I am not one to be a shrew,
But even my storm can't blow these flowers askew.
We bloom together with light spread.
Their tobacco mosaic grounds me more than I could have
said.
The garden we harvest makes a delectable stew.

My heart goes out to the fruitful assortment.
Beautiful apples on a stack of produce.
When looked under a microscope does one see the aston-
ishment
Of a gorgeous, waxy mirror turned to ice with one excuse.
All like the others, frightened of the knife of a single state-
ment.
To buy it, it will seduce.

Squirrels

I am the farmer of my dreams
I see little ones every day
There's evidence of this in the Piazza's towers
I sit down
Or when I feel I need an extra coffee I lay in the grass in
front of Oliphant
The grass tickles me with ambition to get back up
The elephant of this patch pokes me in the butt
"Go on child," mother says
"You've got more studying ahead.
I am here when you need a mother's heart"

Heart Pillow

Have you seen my heart pillow?
The one of many, sentimental
My heart has been woven
With thoughts for a mother
But given to me, or I'd rather say stolen

This heart is carefully woven
And the yarn, carefully chosen.
But when looked at closely,
There seem to be holes
I interweave my fingers throughout
Just so that it can feel
Like maybe you would know in your soul
My fingers wiggle
But they cannot feel a core.

I leave my pillow at sunrise
Ponder about it throughout my day
I remember it is only fluff,
But can't help think it is a disguise
For something I can rest on and decay
Or even hold for comfort so I feel its scruff
Are you indeed my heart pillow?

The Ace of Cups

I'd rather leave my cup outside
Rusting, dirtying, feeding the birds
Than have a chip in my china
I wonder if you notice the stains you left on the sides and
rim
Now don't get too excited,
Nature's lemons will get this clean

Then will I have my five rivers flowing
I hope for this to feed the moss
That one day shall overgrow me
Or surround me to become a pond
I will let ducks, and toads, and butterflies spawn in and
around
And I will feed many flowers
When I finally am outside
How excited I am to be that rusting can

Time

Far and wide,
Yet still never there.
Sweet moments make the two of yours collide
Sour turnings influence as if with no care.
Waiting, waiting, waiting.
Wait.
It's not there.

Unpredictable As...

Unpredictable as a groundhog
Who might not tell the weather.
Unpredictable as a report card
For the quarter.
Unpredictable as auto correct
For sent text messages.
Unpredictable as an iPhone
And its battery level over time.
Unpredictable as a poem
Getting written.

Bryant Leaver

POSTCARD

Dear Baby,

Welcome to the world! In the coming years, you will cry a lot, and Mom will blame you for causing her to go partly deaf in one ear for the rest of your life...

I wish I could sleep and cry as much as you, with it still being socially acceptable. Enjoy it while it lasts. After a certain age, you start getting weird looks.

So much awaits for you so grab your milk bottle and hop on this ride we call life.

Sincerely,
Future you

Bryant Leaver

Mom's arms

2006

POSTCARD

Dear Bry,

Sorry for the long wait since my last letter. Unfortunately, I didn't have much to say to you before the age of 7.

This is a big year for little you, though! Mom and Dad moved the family to a new town after all. Making new friends will be a challenge but I promise you will get there eventually.

This town has its ups and downs, and honestly, you will outgrow it. However, that means bigger things await for when you finally leave. Just give it a good 10 years or so...

See you again in a few years.

Sincerely,
Future you

Bryant Leaver

A new home

2013

POSTCARD

Dear Little Theater Kid,

Hey, you found a new hobby! BEAT Children's Theatre has had a huge impact on your life and it all started with you. Being a performer will continue to give you so much confidence and inspire you to dream big.

Don't let getting cast in minor roles get you down. Soon, you will earn those lead roles and someday, even assistant direct with BEAT.

Soak in every moment and remember to thank Mom and Dad for driving you to rehearsal every day. I look back at these days with fond memories of shows and the friends I made.

Sincerely,
Future you

Bryant Leaver

On stage

2016

POSTCARD

Dear Middle Schooler,

I have so much nostalgia for your life for some reason. I can still remember the crisp, warm air entering the room on a summer morning.

They say that you see the world more vibrant as a kid and fittingly I think my color left around 2020. You'll soon see why.

But don't worry, your life is not all gloom after this year ends! In fact, it is probably just my rose-colored glasses, jealous that you are old enough to do basically whatever you want without worrying about responsibilities yet.

Sincerely,
Future you

Bryant Leaver

Living in a dream

2019

POSTCARD

Dear High Schooler,

Welcome! High school will come with ups and downs but trust me, it is WAY better than middle school.

Prepare to make so many new friends, some good for you and some bad. Prepare to work much harder in school than ever before. But you got this! Finally, prepare to dress much better too.

And don't worry, the pandemic will end in a year. Use the alone time to improve your skills, find new passions, and grow as a person. Your new cat, Marvel, will keep you company.

Sincerely,
Future You

Bryant Leaver

In a zoom meeting

2020

POSTCARD

Dear Explorer,

Looking back on high school, 2021 was my favorite year. I'm not sure why because as I'm writing this, I can only really remember a handful of memorable things you really did.

I think it might be my favorite year because you were starting to figure it all out. Friends, identity, goals in life. We weren't a kid anymore. As an adult now, thank you for fostering what we are today.

Not everything in life will stick but the things that do will last forever.

Sincerely,
Future you

Bryant Leaver

Growing

2021

POSTCARD

Dear Academic Weapon,

This year is really a transformative one for you. Reaching out to BEAT for a position in their organization is the best decision you made. You have so many amazing experiences from it and my resume is thanking you for helping us get the ball running.

Also, you went bungee jumping! We go skydiving in a few years so stay tuned for that.

Additionally, I apologize on behalf of 2021 us for making us take so many AP classes. Taking AP Bio was not necessary in the long run... However, your hard work overall will pay off for graduation.

Keep at it.

Sincerely,
Future you

Bryant Leaver

Jumping off a bridge

2022

POSTCARD

Dear Exhausted Performer,

Yeah, we both know this year is a rough one. You finally leave the choir program because of the teacher. You feel misunderstood by your peers afterward and everyone criticizes your choices.

A year later, he is fired for abusive and predatory behaviors towards students. Good on you for being courageous and making hard choices for yourself. They failed you but there is more to life than setbacks during high school.

Bigger and better things await.

Sincerely,
Future You

Bryant Leaver

Disneyland Jazz choir trip

2023

POSTCARD

Dear Valedictorian,

Congratulations! Truly, you earned it. Your hard work paid off and the life you've waited for is just around the corner.

This year has been the craziest year yet and countless dreams came true. You finally leave the country and discover your passion of traveling. Additionally, you start your first relationship! While you won't find love, you will learn how to love yourself more.

I'm so proud of you.

Sincerely,
Future You

Bryant Leaver

Everywhere

2024

POSTCARD

Dear Me,

Hi there! Working on your postcards,
I see? It's pretty cool that these
will be published in a book.

2025 just started so I don't have too
much to say to you, but I think we
have a lot in store for this year.

I believe this year will be the year
of new opportunities. Working with
Simply Youth Institute is one great
instance.

I'm excited to see what 2025 holds in
store for us.

Sincerely,
Present you

Bryant Leaver
____
writing postcards
____
2025
____
____

POSTCARD

Dear Graduate,

Congratulations again! It feels like we just did this but here you are again.

I wonder what majors and minors you end up with, and from what school. You have a job, right? Or a least a really, really cool internship?

I'm sure you have a lot on your plate, so I won't take too much more time. Even though I am technically an adult already, I feel like adulthood truly starts with you.

Best of luck.

Sincerely,
Past you

Bryant Leaver

Making adult money

2028

POSTCARD

Dear 30 year old,

Wow, life is getting serious, isn't it? I have big expectations for you.

I hope you have your own house. Yes, in this economy it's difficult, but maybe it improves?

I hope that you're married by now. Or at least in a happy long-term relationship. So far, we have not met the one. But I believe in us.

Finally, I hope that you have kids. I'm thinking 2. I am beyond excited to meet your family. Tell him hi for me.

Sincerely,
Past you

Bryant Leaver

A big house

2036

POSTCARD

Dear Grandpa,

By now, I imagine that you to have grandkids. I look forward to having the opportunity to be present in their lives, unlike ours. Give them gifts. Take them on trips. Most importantly, tell embarrassing stories about their Mom or Dad to them.

Surely, you are retired by now too. How incredible it must feel to have so much freedom. But also perhaps quite boring if you have nothing to do.

Maybe that's something I don't fully understand yet... the peace that comes with complete simplicity. I'm learning more every day.

Sincerely,
Past you

Bryant Leaver

Living simply

2080

POSTCARD

Dear Old Man,

I'm not positive that this letter will be delivered to you. But if it does, congratulations on reaching 100 years old!

I hope life has been everything and more that you ever could have wanted. I try to live it to its fullest so you won't have any regrets.

And I hope that you aren't in too much pain. With that, this is my last letter.

I love you.

Sincerely,
Past you

Bryant Leaver

At the end

2106

Lily Petz

A Need to Fall

Most of life is spent
Not allowing myself to fall

Training wheels for bikes
Railings for stairs
Salt for ice
Watching my feet
As to not trip

All ways to avoid
A misstep or slip
To catch my unbalanced self
Before I hit the ground

But then eventually
It's inevitable

I miss the railing
Take off the training wheels
Trip on a rock

And gravity pounces me
Dragging me toward the Earth
Without a cushion
Or anything I can do
But allow myself to lose
To fall

An unforgiving
Scary
Fall
One I am not familiar with

But those moments

After the ground absorbs me
Are the moments that matter

Not all the moments I stopped myself before
But the moment I decided whether to get back up
Or stay down

There is a need to fall
So I can know
If I have the ability
The will power
To gather myself
And continue on

A Sisterhood

I am a Best Friend

And Elle is mine. She is my only friend and I am hers. She is my first friend and I am hers.

We giggle in our shared room under the covers with flashlights long after mommy and daddy tell us goodnight. We ride bikes down the driveway onto the sidewalk until we reach the big tree. We ride up and then down the neighbor's loopy driveway until we reach the blue house. These markings create our kingdom. Everything within it is ours to explore. We explore the roly polys under the rocks and squirm when we see movement under the dirt. We explore the backyard where Cooper lays in the sun waiting for us to play fetch. We explore the Lily flowers that line our driveway allowing the yellow pollen to stain our favorite white shirts.

I am a Protector

We pack our barbies into the pink miniature jeep and drive them down to the front yard for a beach day. Mom has a small pool waiting for us filled with water for the barbies to swim in. While she is playing, Elle jumps into the water slipping and sliding, getting her pretty pink dress all wet. Mom comes out, catching Elle before she slips onto her head and makes more of a mess. Mom gets mad, but not at Elle. She is mad at me for not watching her. From then on I always watch her.

I watched her at the big pool one day. The big pool where we are playing on the stairs together until I get out to rest. The big pool where the lifeguard gets distracted. The big pool where Elle ventures too far into the deep end. The big pool where Elle starts to wave her arms. The big pool where Elle goes motionless, sinking to the tiled floor. The big pool where I jump in and swim as quickly as I can until I reach Elle. The big pool where I grab Elle's skinny arm and pull her to the surface of the water before it is too late. The big pool where I promise Elle I will always protect her.

I am a Caretaker

Elle and I play tag in our backyard in the green grass under the sweet August sun. We dance throughout the garden as I taunt her because I am faster, because Elle cannot catch up. As she runs with all her might at me, she trips on the root of the big tree. Her knee is bleeding as she screams, Mom comes out and she doesn't seem too happy. She isn't mad at Elle, but at me for not taking care of her. At me for not being more careful. From that moment on I will always take care of her.

We load up the car for an adventure up north. Daddy drives while Mommy sews while Elle sleeps while I look out the window thinking of all the fun things we are going to do. When we get to Grandma's cottage she gives us bikes to ride into town. I lead Elle down the big hill telling her to pedal back and use her brakes so as to not go too fast. Elle loses control as her pedals start to spin faster and faster. She speeds past me. Her little legs trying to keep up as the streamers on her bike flap violently in the wind until they stop abruptly.

Until everything stops abruptly.

The world stops as Elle's vulnerable body flies over her handlebars onto the concrete. I sit in frozen shock and fear forcing myself to do something, anything. I run to her aid because I will always take care of her. I comfort her screams of agony as blood streams from her mouth because I will always take care of her. I walk her up the big hill back to Grandma's house, never letting her trembling hand out of my grasp because I will always take care of her.

I am a Stranger

And Elle is too. We do not share giggles under the covers anymore. If I am lucky we share a small glance as we walk past each other in the packed high school hallways. Of course I see her during family dinners, but we rarely speak, and when we speak we fight, and when we fight Mom and Dad fight, and suddenly our family dinners have become less and less. We are both on the swim team, yet I go to practice and Elle skips. When Mom asks me if Elle went to practice today I lie and say she did even though she went to a friend's house instead. I don't know why I still lie for her. I still feel I need to protect her. I miss her, but I don't think she misses me.

I am a Big Sister

And Elle, my little sister.

She came home crying from a party and she wouldn't talk to Mom or Dad. For the first time in a long time, she only wanted to talk to me. I went upstairs to our no longer shared room, as she wept to me about her "close friends" who turned out to not be much of friends at all. I slept in her bed as we shared tears and giggles long after Mom and Dad had gone to bed. We shared memories and regrets. I held Elle until the early morning because I promised I would always take care of her. Because I am her first friend, and she is mine, because I am her best friend and she is mine because I will always be there for her, because I am her big sister.

Homesickness

Homesickness is an interesting feeling, especially as someone who couldn't wait "to get out". I looked down on those who stayed in-state when I first committed to Oregon. Coming from Michigan I was going all the way across the country to be different, to go to a college where I didn't know anyone or anything, but that's what I wanted. It's what I thought I wanted at least. The first term went almost to plan. I had a few bumps in the road of course, but I was making friends, joining a sorority, clubs, and on paper having the best time ever. As the term neared weeks eight and nine, I think the newness was wearing off and I was ready to come home. I missed my mom, my dad, my little sister, my boyfriend, I missed regularity, the mundane. I missed knowing everyone. Still I thought this was just the average feeling of being exhausted from school and ready to just go on winter break.

No one told me coming back is like being jolted awake. Like a dream of falling. It's not as easy to fall back into the swing of things when I spent what felt like endless days and nights filled with the laughter of familiar voices. I sit here now balling my eyes out, wishing I was anywhere but here. Wishing I was home.

I made such a big deal about leaving and not being like everyone else that now I feel like a fool. I am stuck. Staying here, I'm miserable but going back, I'm a failure. What's worse?

Running from Rain

I used to run
Run from the rain
Rain that I wouldn't allow to touch my skin
Skin that had gone through so much already that I ran
Ran from the rain

Why couldn't I?
Why wouldn't I?
Let the rain touch me
It couldn't really hurt me
Right?

This used to be normal
Normal to not want to get wet
Wet from the rain so we bundled up
Up in jackets and boots staying in
In when the sky looked gray
Gray enough that it would rain

Now that I am here no one is scared
Scared of the water that falls from the sky

No one runs
No one even bats an eye
No umbrellas
No hoods
No boots in sight
Just people
Embracing the rain

I used to run
Run from the rain

I still run

Run
Dance
Laugh
Play
In the rain
Just like everyone else here

I let it wash over me because I know
I know there is light coming soon
So for now I enjoy the rain

What is Beauty?

Mirrors consume me
I cannot pass one without a quick glance
A glance that should've taken 5 seconds
Turns to 5 hours
Turns to days upon days
Mirrors upon mirrors

Picking and prying till my face turns red
Body checking and falling into deep dark thoughts
Until I am sitting on my floor crying
Telling myself to never eat again

I try to search for
To find what makes me beautiful
What anyone could ever like
Or even love
Yet I find nothing

When I'm not looking at my own body
My own face
I'm looking at others
Comparing myself to them

Telling myself
If I just stop eating I will look like them
If I just use the right skincare
I will look like them

If you were to ask me
What makes them beautiful
I would not be able to define it

If you were to ask me to
To compare
The beauty of

This girl or that
This flower or that one

I would not be able to

Who am I to compare them?
Who am I to say one is better than the other?
I falsely say
"Everyone is beautiful"

Which I know is a lie
Because if it were true
I would be able to confidently say
I am beautiful

Which
When I am picking and prying
Starving and restricting
Staring in the mirror for hours
I cannot

I wish I could
I do not want to be this way
I wish to see the beauty I find in others
In myself
And some days I do

But maybe one day
I will see my own beauty
Everyday

Jessalyn Beninati-Bautista

Dance: In the Beginning

During the early years of exploring my interests, I always loved going to the Alaska Center for the Performing Arts Center in Anchorage, Alaska. This performing arts center was more of a home to me than the house I grew up in at times. Stepping into the theatre made me feel comfortable and eager as I anticipated the performances I would experience. From early on I knew that my strongest interest in extracurriculars was dance. My mom decided to put me into a gymnastics and dance studio when I was 3 years old. This allowed me the opportunity to explore my interests by participating in a range of classes including; tap, ballet, jazz, and gymnastics. Through this explorative time, I realized that although I may not know exactly which type of dance I was interested in, I knew that it was something I truly enjoyed and looked forward to every day after school.

Over time I found myself drawn to ballet as it became my greatest strength out of all of the types of dance and gymnastics I had tried. Ballet felt natural to me and when I attended my ballet classes I knew it was meant to be. I fell in love with ballet at that moment, including the movement, clean lines, history, and overall beauty I saw. Because of my strong desire to attend ballet classes at my local dance school, I decided to ask my mom if there was any way to continue in ballet. By the age of five, I was placed into a pre-professional ballet studio in Anchorage where I would begin the long journey of my dance career.

As things progressed, my mom enrolled me in a ballet-based company that had a more rigorous approach than the one prior. I began taking dance seriously. I can remember how black the sky would get within the time of one class period and how I could never remember the car ride home due to exhaustion. Every class I took, I grew to love ballet more and more and eventually it was my only interest. Other kids would be trying every recreational sport or hobby out there while my first and last hobby remained dance. I never pursued any other sport because I knew my heart was in dance and dance was what I wanted. From a very young age, I learned what determination and persistence meant and used these qualities as tools to advocate for myself to continue pursuing what I loved. Learning these valuable lessons came straight from my mother. She supported my path and dreams by allowing my journey of exploration and encouraging me to continue attending dance classes.

Moving to Oregon

When I was 7 years old my mom and I decided to move to Oregon to begin a new chapter in our lives. Having the opportunity to move from Alaska to Oregon proved impactful for both of us. When planning our move my mom made sure to find a town that provided the three most important factors for me; education, opportunities, and community. These three foundations have influenced me greatly and I am thankful every day for what my mom did to ensure a solid future.

Having grown up in Alaska, there were limited sources of opportunity and higher education. My mom wanted what was best for me and if that meant moving to a new state and a change in environment for the betterment of my future, and hers, we would push through. Even if pushing through included difficulty in adapting. As I transitioned into this new stage of my life, I also transitioned into a pre-professional ballet studio in Portland. The change began to fully solidify what I wanted in my future and gave me a taste of what it is like to be part of a busy, semi-professional environment.

Dance As My Medium

Throughout my path in dance I have realized that dance is not only an art medium. Dance is a way of speaking and individual expression that gets through to an audience in a different way. Without having to physically talk, audience members can interpret each movement in a way that resonates and feels good to them. This exact epiphany made me think about how much more there is to dance other than labeling it as a form of art. I feel comfortable expressing and advocating for myself and the community for better, which has led me to change paths and truly make an impact.

First Lesson in the Studio

During my first few years at the studio, I found that being open to new teaching and techniques in the classroom allowed me to adapt more easily within the unknown territory I was slowly learning to navigate. I gained many close relationships with my peers and my first mentor. At the time, I did not realize how pivotal my mentor would be in my life. Jason was a great first mentor and there is nothing I would change about our relationship. He taught me that my insecurities were an inner battle. I have always been a timid individual and entering a new studio amplified that feeling. Jason taught me that there was no excuse for feeling insecure and timid and to remind myself that I deserved to be at the studio as much as my peers.

He taught me that I truly was a great and high-quality dancer. This gave me confidence that the art form I love was not something that I needed to question myself or feel insecure about. His support carried through my middle school years as he taught at both my ballet studio and the art school where I attended later on. I would begin to dance over twenty hours a week through my middle and high school years. Looking back, I now view this as my first experience of networking and reflect on how the experience led me to continue to grow and maintain relationships with those I meet as they can lead not only myself, but others into beautiful and meaningful opportunities for the future.

Dancing in High School

As I came to the end of my middle school years I had to decide if continuing my art and passion, or pursuing a higher and rigorous education, is what I needed for my future. During my last year of middle school, I toured private high schools recommended for their ability to prepare students for more prestigious colleges and careers. I was conflicted when my letters of acceptance came in the mail and I decided that the best way of choosing a school was to speak with my mentors and people I looked up to the most. I made plans to meet with Jason and Kemba who have both pursued dance their entire life. They had always acknowledged the importance of having a good education no matter what path I decided to take in life. Conversing with them, creating a list of pros and cons for both scenarios.

Ultimately, I decided that my heart lies with dance. I reminded myself that I would be able to apply the persistence and determination I had used throughout my life if I choose to pursue higher education in the future. My mentors reminded me that although we do have desires and passions, life can change quickly. What we learn during life is important and those lessons can be applicable to all of my pursuits.

During my high school years I increased participation in my dance career by becoming part of the art school's dance team. This opportunity led me to perform and give back to my community. I volunteered for local companies, including the Oregon Symphony. I raised money for my school, partnered with international dance companies to embrace the arts in my hometown, and traveled across the country to represent my high school at national dance festivals. Through these events, I have been approached by many young children who shared with me how much I have inspired them to start dancing. These children's praise was solely based on my presence as an Asian in a predominantly white community. I have realized that many young girls see themselves in me when I perform on stage.

Growing up, I didn't see many Asian representations of female dancers. Dancing for a young audience allowed me to change children's perspectives of who belongs on the stage. I felt assured that I had done what I hoped to for my community by making an impact. I never had a role model that represented my cultural background, and I am glad that I can be a figure to look up to for the next generation. Although I have changed my career path, I feel that this learning experience still applies to me in every aspect of my life. Being a leader for my community who motivates youth to become our future leaders encourages me to push the limits. I want to be the best version of myself and give back to my community.

College Years

During my first year of college I found the environment intimidating at first. Over time, I realized that the University of Oregon had widened my perspective through the support of my friends, people from diverse backgrounds. I was able to view college as an opportunity to grow and explore rather than allow myself to revert back to the timid girl I was before. I felt like an imposter taking a spot as a student at my university when I knew there may have been hundreds of students more qualified than me. Harder working than me. I reminded myself of the lessons I had learned throughout my life and that I deserved to be at the university. Uncomfortable at first, I pushed myself to learn to love and appreciate the lessons education offered me.

I knew that the best way to acclimate at the university was to find a community that I identified closely with, felt comfortable with, especially coming from a high school that had little Asian representation. I began to attend the Asian Pacific American Student Union and Korean Student Association club meetings weekly, and I soon made many friends who I strongly connected with on a cultural level. APASU announced a new program for the fall of 2022. The program paired upperclassmen with first year students as mentors and guides. The mentors were provided to students to help people navigate the "ways" of the university and was called the "big little" program. As a first year, my mentor helped me overcome my feelings of intimidation in college and introduced me to more people within the Asian community.

My second year, I decided to sign up to be a "big" freshman through the "big little" program. I enjoyed building connections with my assigned freshmen and watching them grow and become a part of the community on campus. Having the ability to guide incoming students through their time at U of O's education and community inspired me to give even more back to the community. This is something which has made me feel comfortable within my culture and ethnicity. As I continued to explore pursuits outside of dance, I found that I was drawn to medicine and I began to explore how I could make an impact within mental health as a doctor.

Transitioning from dance to medicine hasn't dampened my commitment to make an impact. My focus remains on shaping the perspectives of the next generation, fostering inclusivity and mental health. I aim to instill in children the belief that the impossible is achievable, guiding them toward a brighter and healthier future.

My Future

Now, in my third year of college, I have a renewed passion for dance and have added a minor in dance to my degree program. I have learned many important lessons from my dance career that I apply to all aspects of my life. I would not change anything about my past because it has led to such an enriched path in life through the people who have played large, supporting, roles. I have been given many opportunities and as I continue to pursue a pre-med path with a major in psychology, I have the opportunity to intern abroad at a cancer research hospital in Italy where I will continue to improve my skills and gain new professional skills in global health.

I am beginning to plan my future goals. After I graduate I will explore new interests I did not know I had until my college experience in dance. I plan to continue in academia by working on a masters of science in global public health. I have always been passionate about providing opportunities for underserved populations. I am privileged to have personal experiences with my family members who have immigrated from the Philippines as they relate their stories to me. I find it important to fight against the inequality of treatment around the world.

As a student, I am fortunate to get to attend classes and experience the healthcare field abroad. This will set me up for success as a physician and is a great first step in forming my passion into supporting underserved populations. Looking back, I see that my life has taught me to prepare for what I want in my future by allowing me to continuously pursue my interests, involve myself in those interests, and continue to be proactive and disciplined in providing a more impactful future for my community.

College Decisions

After reaching the turning point and realizing how I truly view dance made me think about what I wanted to do in my future. Seeing the impact I made in my community, inspiring children to follow the same dreams I had as a child, I knew I wanted to make a larger impact beyond my hometown. When the pandemic of 2020 shut down schools and establishments all over the world, I began to become interested in mental health. During sophomore and junior year in high school, I watched many Americans across the country as they began to speak out about the importance of mental health during the prolonged isolation. As I continued to read more about mental health and realized what many of my loved ones were experiencing, it led me to want to pursue something that would help.

I became more interested in how I could make a change and aid my loved ones from a distance. I also began to think about children as young as my little cousins, missing out on pivotal moments in their life. I had the opportunity to experience those moments pre-pandemic, and I realized how detrimental it is not to have the personal and physical connection with people in the community. Because of this, I began to have long, meaningful conversations with my mom about the importance of mental health. As my biggest supporter, she encouraged me to pursue psychology at the University of Oregon which led me to pursue a career as a pediatric psychiatrist.

By my senior year of high school, we had begun full in-person attendance again and I continued to dance until I graduated. Before graduation, I had my senior capstone project. I had researched extensively and finally presented it to student guests. I spoke about my own personal growth in high school and advocated for the importance of mental health support. I had the artistic freedom to create a

performative piece that allowed me to express myself and
tell my story through the medium I had learned to commu-
nicate through. Dance.

My Mother

From a very young age my mom has been my idol in every aspect of my life. She has taught me several lessons and overall perspectives of life. She was a single mother raising her only child and I observed in her a consistent resilience and strength that I have and continue to look up to everyday. She has taught me how to advocate for myself in what I like and dislike and not be ashamed of my opinions, rather to speak loud enough to make an impact and create an identity for myself.

Throughout my life my mother has played a major supporting role in how I carry myself today as well as at the start of my dancing career. She has encouraged me to explore and experience everything that I find interesting and has pushed me to, at least, try everything once even if I felt intimidated by how intense something seemed. I have idolized my mom for what she has taught me and demonstrated throughout my life. I have seen the resilience she had as a single mom. She raised me on her own and pushed her way through every aspect of life no matter her identity.

My relationship with my mom has created a safe space for me to express myself without caring about the pressure of societal norms and to have open conversations while having opposing opinions. By setting up a reality based perspective of society, I was able to develop a belief that although society may not agree with me all the time, I still have the ability to have my own identity and beliefs. Having this strength has allowed me to build an attitude of communication with the people around me, creating a safe space for my peers, room for us to express ourselves without judgement, and the ability to support each other in different ways.

Mentors Matter

I am grateful everyday for growing up in the best environment possible for expanding my opportunities not only in dance, but in my overall life. Relationships are valuable to me. Both the relationships I have with my family, and those with my mentors and friends, are pivotal in my life. The people who continued to stand beside me when I decided to change course in college, from dance to medicine, will always hold a place of value in my life. I am continuously reminded of the people who have helped guide me and I work as hard as I can to celebrate my accomplishments with them. With their guidance, I have been able to pursue everything I put my mind to, just like my family taught me.

I value the determination that has been instilled in me by microsystems and the environments I was placed in where I could work hard to reach the desires I wanted for my future. By spending several hours a day with my dance teachers, both in school and the studio, my relationship with teachers were strengthened. Knowing that they cared about more than just my performance in class meant a lot to me and helped guide me to a place of belonging in the studio. My dance teachers Jason Davis and Kemba Shannon have taught me many lessons, teaching me how standing with confidence opens many doors and creates traction towards the creative outlets and passions, both dance and other interests outside of extracurriculars. These amazing people taught me valuable lessons that I plan to apply throughout the rest of my life.

I have learned the importance of having mentors who have years of life experience. My mentors have given me incredible support and perspective that they wished they had earlier in life and they wanted to support me in achieving a bright future. My mentors are dear to me and I admire them greatly. I constantly remind myself that the goals

I am working toward are also for the people who have also helped me get to where I am now.

Marlene Beltran Ruiz

The Power of Dreams

Dreams all start midway.
They never have a beginning,
it just keeps going
until you wake up.

Mine start like movie scenes
and are forever changing.
It can change like flipping
through channels on television.

A different plot and characters
in the blink of an eye.
I will dream of something horrible
and my mind will stay in that scene
for what feels like an eternity.

I feel dread hoping my dream will change.
Instead the dread turns to fear
and spreads throughout my body.

I would dream of a car ride driving home
feeling eyes on me and turning trying to see
what is looking at me and seeing a Porcelain doll.

Then I would turn forward feeling those eyes
closer to me then before, almost touching me.

I would go into my home feeling
Something is following me,
like I can't get away.

Every time I look for this bad feeling
I would see this doll getting closer and closer,
trying to get to me.

I know something is wrong.
I want to wake up.
I try to tell myself that this is a dream

but there is a force keeping me there.
I want to change the dream but it's futile.
I turn to tell someone what is happening;
I feel total and utter shock.

I am able to open my eyes,
I'm grateful I'm awake
and none of it was real.

I would dream about
something exciting and happy
right when it goes to the good
part of my brain changes the setting.

I would dream about a school dance
with a boy I don't know.
He is looking at me with eyes so bright,
I wonder what he was thinking.

Then he would smile and spin me around and around.
I would feel that thrill of exhilaration,
praying the moment would last forever.

I woke up sad that it had to end.
I want to fall back asleep
just to go back to that moment
and appreciate a wonderful feeling.

Dear Hair,

You and I have been through quite the Journey. Ever since I was little, I was told that I needed to have you long to be considered beautiful. I looked at other girls with short hair, and thought, "how cute!" When I asked my father if I could cut you short. He would tell me "Not too short, or it's going to look ugly." "I like how you look with long hair." As the years went by you changed, from straight with slight wave to wonderful curls. I allowed you to grow, because with each passing day people would stop to tell me how beautiful you are. They would ask me "Is it Fake?" "Is it real?" "Where do you get your hair?" I let them know you are real and all mine. Then I would see dyed hair, short hair, and bald, all worn proudly. I would be green with envy, wanting the choice to do what I want with you. I had a friend who would do all types of crazy things with her hair, she would change the length and dye it all of the colors of the rainbow. I finally gathered the courage to ask for a change. My mother agreed readily but my father was a different matter completely. Resistant to change. I was determined to finally have the opportunity to make a choice for myself. It started out small. I dyed your tips blue, then as you grew, I dyed more and more of you, changed your colors until color was half of you. The constant work I put into you started to change you. You were no longer vibrant, soft, healthy. You become brittle and broke easily, no longer having your beautiful curl. I needed to cut out the damaged parts of you. I got you cut below my shoulders. I had a burst of excitement in my chest finally seeing you something other than long, I didn't realize how much you would shrink. When I got home with my hair freshly washed, you rose above my shoulders. My father exploded, "Why is it so short?!"

"I can't even look at you!" When he uttered those words I wanted to cry. Excitement twisted into fear and sadness. When I woke up the next day you had curled so much, you were right by my chin. I loved how you looked, I didn't care how upset anyone was. I had already made the change. I allowed you to grow, but there was this itch under my skin to change you. It was a siren call that became louder and louder as time passed. I shaved the side of you, the bottom of you, and finally I wanted to completely remove you. Everyone questioned me or thrust their opinion on me. "Why do you keep cutting your hair?" "You would look so pretty with longer hair." "You look so boyish with short hair." "Your hair was better long." Why does it matter to others if I changed you? You were mine to do whatever I wanted with. I didn't care how others looked at you. I only cared about how you made me feel. You had a direct connection with my emotions. If you were unsightly, I was annoyed or discombobulated. If you looked phenomenal, I was confident to downright cocky. I came to realize the reason that I loved changing you so much is because you were the one thing that was mine and mine alone. You were the one thing I could control in my life if nothing else.

Sincerely,

Me

Dear Boy With The Chocolate Eyes,

I liked you when we were young, but I could not tell you.
I did not believe you would ever like me. I believed that I
was ugly and not pretty enough to be liked. I thought I was
too boyish and loud to be liked. I thought I was too aggres-
sive to be considered a girl. I was not like other girls, so I
thought no one would like me. You were tall, funny, a nice
guy. You were always considerate of others, made them feel
included. You were surrounded by friends and I was one
of them. I was happy with just that. At least I can talk with
you. I knew all of the girls in our friend group had a crush
on you, I was just another one. But I would never admit it,
let the other girls do that. I had a different way of express-
ing my feelings. Instead of telling you or treating you well,
I was mean to you. I made fun of you to the point you got
annoyed. I would worry I went too far, and just stop talking
to you. Before I could get into my head about it you would
talk and joke around with me. I was fine until you asked me
to the dance. I said yes. In my head we were just going as
friends. Someone got it into my head that you liked me, I
denied it. I couldn't let myself believe that you could ever
want me, but there was a swelling in my heart with want.
I tried not to let it get to my head. All of it was for nothing
because my heart still broke when you got a girlfriend.
I felt stupid for even believing you could like me. When
you broke up with her, I knew better than to want to. My
heart did not get the message, I had to remind myself there
was no one who would want me. Time went and noth-
ing happened. We were on our way to adulthood leaving
behind blissful adolescence. We were graduating and I
told you that my best friend wanted you to be her first kiss
and I could tell in your face, you were so thrown off. You
couldn't believe those words were uttered out of my mouth.
When the time came, you couldn't do it and I was so upset.
But when it came to me, you were so ready and I was flab-

bergasted "how? How could it be that you want me?" I was
mad. You were left wondering what the hell just happened.
We still hung out as friends and one night you decided to
ask me if I was willing to fool around with you. How could
I miss my chance and you said to keep it a secret from
everyone else? It hurt my heart, but I was willing to keep it
history. Because I knew the other girls had a crush on you
too. So it came to my surprise when days later there were
girls blowing up my phone telling me how dare you how
could you be really a friend. Then I get a call from my best
friend who had a crush on you too saying why did I keep it
a secret? Why didn't I tell her anything? The reason I didn't
tell anyone was because you told me not to. I decided then
that I couldn't trust you, and there was no point, I needed to
move forward, even if I still liked you. Years later, I finally
understood. You were a young boy and you had a joyous
moment. You wanted to enjoy it, share it with someone and
of course you couldn't help it. What I didn't realize is how
much I would want to relish what happened. It was a grat-
ifying moment. So much feeling. I felt overwhelmed. But
I had to keep it to myself, and I could not share in the joy.
That moment ended and became a memory.

Sincerely,

Me

Arielle Villalpando

Coffee Date With Grandma

I could sit here and write about how I would love to have coffee with Ariana Grande or meet with an alien but if I truly could meet anyone for coffee I would meet with an unfiltered version of my grandmother. My grandma is one of the most inspiring, hardworking, and strongest people in my life. She is funny, intelligent, and wise. Her life has been filled with many stories and lessons to share but she is always closed off. My grandmother loves to talk about her kids, her late husband, adventures with her friends, and the novelas she has watched but she rarely mentions stories about herself. My grandma is like a dusty book, placed at the highest corner of the largest library. You could read hundreds of books with similar concepts but they will never be as good as the ones you can not obtain.

I ask her millions of questions but she always avoids the true answer with a change of conversation. I could ask my tías and tíos but they never know the entire story. I was once assigned an oral history project in my AP U.S. History class. We had to interview someone about a significant piece of history in their life. I chose my grandmother. We talked about her immigration story and the struggles she overcame in the working environment. This was one of the few glimpses I've gotten of her life and this only makes me crave more. During this interview, my grandmother gave me two pieces of advice. She told me that although you may experience hardships in life or bumps in the road, it is important to acknowledge what has happened but you must keep moving forward with positivity.

My grandma has had a tough life but she keeps pushing forward with positivity and I believe that makes her resilient. She also expressed that it is important to embrace your culture and your heritage. You must keep it near and dear to your heart because that is the one thing that can always connect you to your ancestors. My grandma can teach me so much about my culture and ancestry and even more about her life but a coffee never stays hot for too long.

The reason I most want to have coffee with an unfiltered version of my grandmother is because I believe that she has a life worth sharing. She has many experiences that can teach me great lessons and change the way I view the world. But most of all, I want to learn every detail of her life in hopes that I will never forget her.

About the Authors

Jacob Long

Jacob is a current media studies and cinema studies major and a freshman enrolled at the University of Oregon, and is passionate about creativity, storytelling, and leadership. As a Simply Youth Institute Intern and social media content creator, he has gotten deeply involved in promoting self-discovery and problem solving for young adults through a video series medium. Jacob has used this opportunity to broaden his skills in content production, storytelling, networking and teamwork, collaborating with fellow interns to work towards the collective goal of promoting peace and prosperity for the youth of Lane County. In this anthology, Jacob features a collection of pieces on his journey towards independence, growth, and self-love. He's not afraid to get personal with his work, encouraging others to reflect on their past experiences and understand the journey towards who they are today. Jacob's pieces encourage readers to recognize that pain is a part of the process in becoming whole, and it's never a bad thing to be vulnerable. Jacob is excited to keep working in the cornerstone of where content creation and storytelling intersects. In his future, Jacob plans to be a documentary producer, discovering monumental and uplifting stories that can be told through the medium of film. He believes that everyone has a story, and he hopes that his writing will encourage others to tell their stories as well.

Skyla Bird

Driven by a deep commitment to environmental sustainability and community empowerment, Skyla Bird brings passion and purpose to her role as a Workforce Readiness Intern at Simply Youth Institute. A junior at the University of Oregon majoring in Environmental Studies with a minor in Music, Skyla combines scientific insight with creative expression to engage and uplift those around her. From leading impactful recycling initiatives at Sedona Recycles to managing the hustle of customer service as a barista and cashier, Skyla's diverse experience reflects her adaptability, leadership, and love for serving others. As a former student body vice president and concertmaster of the Sedona Community Youth Orchestra, she's no stranger to mobilizing people toward a shared vision. She continues to inspire change through climate advocacy and youth-led projects like the award-winning SRRHS Blood Drive. Skyla is excited to bring her collaborative spirit, organizing skills, and environmental consciousness to the SYI team, helping prepare the next generation of changemakers for a bright and bold future.

Anya Grabovski

From a young age, Anya has been inspired by artistic works. Her passion for creativity and symbolism unfolds delicately throughout her featured literary works. As a Business Marketing student, Anya strives to display elaborate and unique forms of symbolism to communicate emotions and story lines. Her journey of self-development and understanding is guided through the selected poetry throughout this anthology. Outside of this anthology, Anya appreciates the outdoors, going to museums, and exploring new mediums to express her artistic passion. She spends her days biking, spending time with friends, and building towards her career in Marketing. As a transfer student from Chapman University and with her diverse travel portfolio, Anya has been able to experience different environments and cultures around the world. These experiences assist her in the poetry featured in this anthology. She aspires to travel and experience new things as her life continues to inspire more art going forward.

Bryant Leaver

Bryant is an advertising and film student with a passion for using compelling visuals and storytelling to promote positivity and meaningful causes. During his internship with Simply Youth Institute, he contributed to the Content Writing, Graphic Design, and Branding team—helping communicate the organization's mission, raise awareness about women's empowerment, and spotlight key events.

In this anthology, Bryant presents a series of postcards addressed to different years of his life. These postcards reflect on the past, explore the present, and imagine the future, weaving a narrative of personal growth and self-discovery. His writing embraces the complexities of growing up—the highs, the lows, and the lessons in between. As the collection progresses, Bryant looks forward to the life that lies ahead, maintaining a tone of hope and optimism. Through these reflections, he encourages readers to examine their own journeys—with both critical thought and heartfelt appreciation—reminding us that while the past shapes who we are, it often feels fleeting in the grand scope of life.

Jessalyn Beninati-Bautista

Jessalyn Beninati-Bautista is a rising leader who brings heart, intellect, and artistry to her role as a Workforce Readiness Intern at Simply Youth Institute. A Psychology major with minors in Chemistry and Dance at the University of Oregon, Jessalyn is passionate about mental wellness, cultural identity, and creative expression—primarily through contemporary dance, her favorite form of storytelling. Her journey reflects a deep dedication to building inclusive, empowered communities. Whether she's mentoring peers through the Asian Pacific American Student Union's Big Little Program or spotlighting cultural pride as a performer with the Korean Student Association, Jessalyn leads with authenticity and warmth. Her experience in leadership, communication, and service makes her a natural fit for creating impactful programming for youth. Jessalyn moves with purpose at every step, whether on stage or in service. She's proud to support young people as they build confidence, resilience, and readiness for their futures.

Lily Petz

Lily Petz is a freshman at the University of Oregon who has enjoyed poetry and storytelling from a young age. She loves using her words to share her story with others and bring hope to those going through the same struggles. It is not always easy sharing with the world, but if it even makes one person feel less alone it will have been worth it. In her free time Lily loves visiting the Great Lakes or her home state Michigan and going on long walks with her dog Cooper.

Marlene Beltran Ruiz

Marlene Beltran Ruiz is a dedicated humanitarian committed to fostering personal growth and meaningful connections through every interaction. Guided by the belief that "actions speak louder than words" and inspired by the mantra "be the change you want to see in the world," she continuously seeks to make a positive impact. Her journey began as a student worker at East Los Angeles College, where she discovered a passion for engaging with and supporting others. Currently working in the healthcare field, Marlene emphasizes the importance of mental health as a vital component of overall well-being, equal to physical health. Having faced and overcome personal challenges as a young adult, she is driven to support and inspire the next generation with the insights she has gained along the way. Outside of her professional endeavors, Marlene enjoys a variety of hobbies including cooking, rollerblading, reading, and watching films. She values quality time with her family and finds solace in connecting with nature. Marlene believes in the importance of pushing oneself toward growth, while also recognizing the essential need for rest and rejuvenation.

Arielle Villalpando

Arielle Villalpando is a passionate Workforce Readiness Intern at Simply Youth Institute, where she channels her love for community and family into meaningful action. Rooted in strong family values, Arielle draws inspiration from the people closest to her, bringing warmth, empathy, and a nurturing spirit to every space she enters. Arielle's leadership is grounded in care and connection. Whether uplifting her peers, supporting youth on their career paths, or organizing impactful initiatives, her approach is always people-first. Her love for family fuels her commitment to building environments where everyone feels supported, heard, and empowered to grow. At SYI, Arielle is proud to help shape a future where young leaders rise confidently and the community feels like home.

Publisher's Note

Daxson publishing was created to help marginalized artists publish their work, so the world can hear their voice. The vision for this publishing house is to help people get their work out there, and not have them struggle finding their way through the publishing process. Everyone's voice deserves to be heard, and we are here to help. If you are interested in submitting a manuscript, email daxsonpublishing@gmail.com. Other books sold at daxsonpublishing.com.